P9-BZR-539

Jan 18

BUILDING
ON A
DREAM

THE
GOLDEN
GATE
BRIDGE

Kayleen Reusser

PURPLE TOAD
PUBLISHING

Printing   1   2   3   4   5   6   7   8   9

Big Ben
The Burj Khalifa
The Eiffel Tower
The Empire State Building
The Golden Gate Bridge
The Great Wall of China

The Leaning Tower of Pisa
The Space Needle
The Statue of Liberty
The Sydney Opera House
The Taj Mahal
The White House

Publisher's Cataloging-in-Publication Data
Reusser, Kayleen.
  Golden Gate Bridge / written by Kayleen Reusser.
    p. cm.
Includes bibliographic references, glossary, and index.
ISBN 9781624693489
1. Golden Gate Bridge (San Francisco, Calif.)—Juvenile literature. 2. Architecture—Vocational guidance—Juvenile literature. I. Series: Building on a Dream: Kids as Architects and Engineers.
 NA2555 2017
 720

Library of Congress Control Number: 2017940645

eBook ISBN: 9781624693496

ABOUT THE AUTHOR: As an author of children's books, Kayleen Reusser has written biographies, STEM books, cookbooks and books about crafts. She has published newspaper and magazine articles on travel, profiles, and history and essays for Chicken Soup. She is working on a series of books on World War II and coordinates two writing clubs. Find out more at www.KayleenReusser.com.

CONTENTS

Marin County

Golden Gate

San Francisco
Peninsula

Joseph Strauss dreamed of building the longest and most beautiful suspension bridge in the world across the Golden Gate Strait.

Big Dreams

Ooga! Ooga! Ooga!

Joseph Strauss looked over the balcony outside his hotel room. Hundreds of people stood on the shore of the Golden Gate Strait, tooting car horns. Some people shouted. Others waved fists. Many of them had already waited hours to ride the ferry across the strait to Marin County.

All day the boats chugged back and forth along the narrow, windy channel. Though the ferry captains skillfully steered their vessels, there were always more people waiting to cross. Strauss didn't have to squint at the faces of those waiting on the shore to know they were red with frustration.

The city of San Francisco sits at the northern end of San Francisco Peninsula. The Pacific Ocean lies to the west, and San Francisco Bay to the east. The 1.7-mile Golden Gate Strait separates the city from Marin County. In 1917, more than 500,000 people lived in San Francisco, famous for its international port.[1]

While San Francisco was a beautiful, exotic city, many people rode the ferries on weekends to escape to the serene countryside of Marin County. There they hiked, picnicked, and relaxed. Many people who lived in Marin County worked in San Francisco. They rode the ferries to work every morning and home again each evening.

Strauss took a deep breath, inhaling the salty sea air. As more people moved to the area, he knew the ferries would become even

more crowded. Driving around the bay was no answer. The journey was nearly 200 miles.

To Strauss the answer was obvious. The city of San Francisco needed a bridge to move people quickly and efficiently across the Strait.

Strauss hired geologists to measure the swirling water's depths, study the tides and currents, and take samples of the bedrock. The results were grim. In some places, the water was more than 400 feet deep. High winds caused ocean tides to rush through the strait. The area, often cool in the morning and warm during the day, was famous for its heavy fog. There was also the threat of earthquakes, as the San Andreas Fault lay nearby.

The bridge would have to be very high over the strait. Otherwise it would interfere with the heavy shipping traffic to and from the port.

As Strauss looked over the Golden Gate Strait, he stood to his full height of five feet, three inches. Joseph Strauss was not a tall man, but he liked to dream big.[2]

Strauss owned a bridge-building company and already had built bridges around the world. He knew a bridge over the Golden Gate Strait would have to be strong to stand against the powerful tides and the strong

The San Andreas Fault extends for 800 miles in California.

In 1895, people traveled by boat across the Golden Gate Strait.

winds that blew in from the Pacific. He would calculate the bridge's dead weight, including roads, railroad tracks, sidewalks, water pipes, signs, and railings. He would also add the amount of live weight from traffic along the bridge—cars, trucks, trains, and people.

Strauss decided the best solution would be a suspension bridge. Suspension bridges are held up by steel cables that run between a pair of towers. They allow for longer spans than other types of bridges. If the Golden Gate Bridge were a suspension bridge, the span could be long enough for ships to pass each other between the two towers.

Strauss worked on his design. He knew if he built a strong, beautiful bridge, people would get to their destinations faster, and visitors would want to see it.

When Strauss shared his idea of building the longest, tallest, strongest, most beautiful suspension bridge in the world, officials in San Francisco thought he was crazy. Maybe he was. Not even Strauss had ever attempted to build a suspension bridge of the size he was proposing.

Could it be done?

Joseph Strauss dreamed of building a bridge like the Cincinnati-Covington Bridge that stretched over the Ohio River. It was renamed the Roebling Bridge in 1983.

CHAPTER 2

"Bridge the Gate"

Joseph Strauss had dreamed of building bridges since he was a boy. Born in 1870, he grew up in Cincinnati, Ohio. He had often admired the Cincinnati-Covington Bridge that stretched over the Ohio River. (In 1983, the bridge was renamed the John A. Roebling Bridge.) With great stone pillars, high towers, and graceful cables, the Cincinnati-Covington Bridge was the first long-span suspension bridge in America. Strauss wanted to build other bridges like it.

Strauss graduated from the University of Cincinnati, then worked for an engineering firm. In 1904, he started his own business—the Strauss Bascule Bridge Company.

Working from a blueprint, Strauss decided the bridge over the Golden Gate Strait would hang from two main cables held up by two towers.

From his experience in building bridges, Strauss knew certain forces would work against those cables. Those forces were compression and tension.

Compression occurs when something is shortened or squeezed, making it smaller. An example of compression is when a person tightens the bicep muscle in his arm. As the muscle is squeezed, it compresses and becomes shorter.

On a bridge the weight of traffic compresses, or pushes down, on the deck. If the weight on the deck becomes too much, the bridge buckles and cracks.

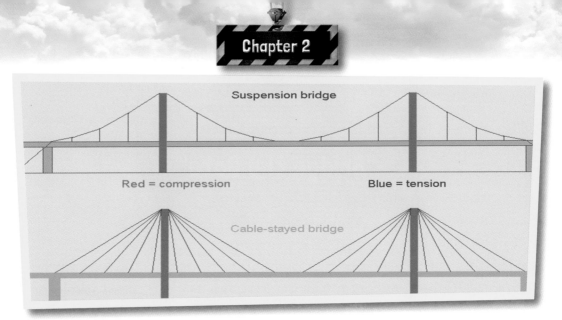

Suspension bridge

Red = compression

Blue = tension

Cable-stayed bridge

Strauss' design for a bridge over the Golden Gate Strait had two towers and suspension cables. The cables would transfer the weight of the bridge to the towers and the ground.

Tension, the force of pulling something apart, is the opposite of compression. Tension can be seen in a game of tug-of-war. When two opposing teams pull on a rope, it becomes taut or tense. If too much weight is loaded on a bridge, tension on the deck can cause it to bend and snap.

The truss framework on the Golden Gate Bridge provided a strong bridge deck.

In a suspension bridge, compression and tension are spread to the cables. The cables are attached to the bridge's anchorages. They, like the towers, are built into the ground. When tension from the cables is directed to the ground, pressure is removed from the bridge.

Suspension bridges are exposed to tremendous pressure. High winds can cause the bridge to twist. This twisting force is

Irving Morrow

called torsion. If torsion is not controlled, it can destroy a bridge.

Strauss planned to combat torsion by using trusses. A truss is a type of framework made of metal or wood that strengthens and holds a structure in place. Trusses on the Golden Gate Bridge would reinforce the bridge's deck, the area where people would walk and drive.

Strauss hired Irving Morrow, an architect from San Francisco, to design the bridge's two towers. Morrow shaped them like tall rectangles. He placed openings in the towers to make the bridge lighter and better able to resist high winds. Morrow's design looked slim, sleek, and modern.

Another challenge would be the length of the bridge's center span. At that time, the Brooklyn Bridge in New York had the longest span in the world. It stretched nearly 1,600 feet between its towers. The Golden Gate Bridge would span 4,200 feet—eight tenths of a mile.

Built in 1883, the Brooklyn Bridge in New York City connected Manhattan and Brooklyn over the East River.

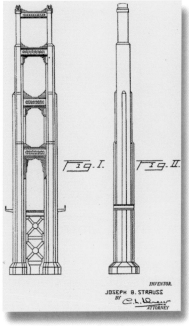

Tower design

Strauss tested the design for the Golden Gate Bridge on a 13-foot steel model. He added 250 pairs of vertical cables to transfer pressure from the bridge to the ground. He researched heavy traffic loads and temperature changes. He also placed the model in a wind tunnel to test its strength against the winds that would howl through the strait.

Based on his research, Strauss finished his design. The Golden Gate Bridge would be supported by concrete towers resting on deep foundations, two main cables, and 250 support cables.

Strauss submitted his bid for a suspension bridge to the San Francisco city engineer in 1921. The cost would be $35 million. When asked who would pay for such an expensive bridge, Strauss said the bridge would pay for itself with tolls.

Military experts worried that naval ships entering or leaving the harbor would collide with the bridge's piers. Strauss explained the towers would have at least a half-mile of space between them. Lights would mark the piers and towers to help sailors see them at night or in foggy weather.

Other people worried about being on the bridge during an earthquake. In 1906, an earthquake struck San Francisco, killing more than 3,000 people. Strauss explained that the

Each of the bridge's two main cables were spun to have a diameter of 36 inches.

San Francisco after the 1906 earthquake

bridge's strength and ability to sway would keep it safe.

Ferry companies opposed the bridge. A bridge would put them out of business.

Government officials in San Francisco believed building the bridge could solve the city's unemployment problem. One in four people were out of work. The bridge project would need workers in mills, mines, and quarries; drivers to haul materials; and road crews. Laborers who lived in the area could earn $11.00 a day.[1]

As time passed, more people liked the idea. They handed out stickers with the words "Bridge the Gate" printed on them.[2]

Finally, in 1928, city officials approved the project. They appointed Strauss as engineer in charge.

Shortly after the design was approved, the country faced a financial crisis. The stock market crashed, companies failed, and many people lost their jobs. Money was scarce. This time in history became known as the Great Depression.

A. P. Giannini, president of the Bank of America, believed the bridge would help San Francisco. It would bring more people to the city, and it would provide jobs. He agreed to loan Strauss the money to build it.

The city of San Francisco would finally have a new bridge.

Top: For the north pier, men worked inside a cofferdam like this one. Bottom: A trestle connected the south pier to the shore.

Construction

Construction on the Golden Gate Bridge began in January 1933. Several years had passed since Strauss first tested the floor of the strait. He needed to know if anything had changed. Deep-sea divers found firm bedrock at the shallow north pier site. At the south side, however, the bottom dropped to 250 feet below the surface of the water. The piers at each end would have to be built differently from each other.

A foundation goes deep into the ground to keep a bridge from toppling over in the wind or sinking under its own weight. Piers are huge towers built on top of foundations.

Strauss started with the pier at the shallow north end. He used bombs planted underwater to break up a large area of rock. When this was removed, it created a level area on which to build the foundation.

Next, Strauss built a large wooden frame called a cofferdam. The sides of the cofferdam were reinforced with steel. As the cofferdam was lowered into the water, the water inside was pumped out. Inside, the cofferdam was a dry, safe place to work.

Day after day, a fleet of trucks poured concrete into the cofferdam. Concrete is a mixture of cement, water, sand, and gravel. It can be poured into molds and shaped into girders and beams. When concrete cures, it becomes strong and hard.

When the weather changes, concrete expands or contracts. These changes can make concrete crack. Pouring wet concrete over steel wires or a grid of steel bars strengthens the concrete and keeps it from

cracking. This reinforced concrete was used in the foundations of the bridge. Then, the piers were poured. The mass of concrete for the bridge's north pier rose 44 feet above the surface of the water.

To work at the south end, Strauss created a roadway over the water called a trestle. It extended 1,100 feet from shore and was strong enough to support cranes and other heavy machinery.

One foggy night a freighter crashed into the trestle. A few months later a storm damaged it. Strauss rebuilt the trestle and used a caisson to keep water out. The caisson looked like a soup can with the bottom cut out. It provided a dry place in which to build the south pier.

For the towers on top of the two piers, workers used powerful cranes to hoist 5,000 steel sections into place. More than one million rivets held the sections together. Workers balanced on beams at

Workers used cranes to hoist heavy steel sections into place.

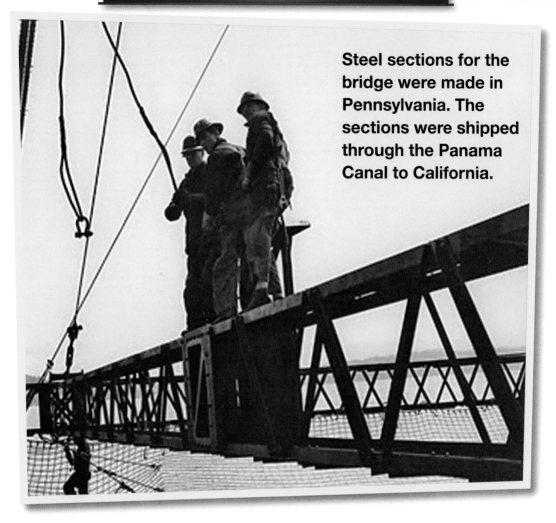

Steel sections for the bridge were made in Pennsylvania. The sections were shipped through the Panama Canal to California.

dizzying heights of up to 746 feet.[1] The people of San Francisco and Marin County watched as the towers grew taller each day over the strait.

Two years had passed since construction on the bridge began. Foundations, anchorages, piers, and towers stood in place, but several months of work lay ahead. The people of northern California wondered, would the world's largest bridge ever be finished?

Huge bolts to fasten supports for the cables were tightened by hand.

Safety on the Bridge

The next step in the bridge's construction was to spin the two main cables. The cables had to be extra strong because they would support most of the bridge's weight. They would also counter the torsion forces caused by high winds.

The business of John Roebling and Sons was hired to spin the cables. Roebling had already spun cables for the construction of other bridges, including the Brooklyn Bridge in New York.

Back and forth, over the two great towers in the middle, from the north anchorage of the bridge to the south, the cables were made. Each wire was less than 0.2 inches in diameter, but the main cables ended up being three feet in diameter. They were 7,659 feet long, and each contained 27,572 individual wires. If placed end to end, the wires within them would reach around the world three times.

As bridge building was risky, Strauss insisted his workers observe safety precautions. Everyone wore hard hats. Men who worked in dangerous places wore safety belts connecting them to something secure. Those who worked in the high towers wore dark glasses to protect their eyes from the glare of sunlight on water.[1] If a man tried to show off as a daredevil, he was fired.[2]

Strauss knew workers on the roadway would be risking their lives as they worked high above the water. Before work on the deck began, Strauss ordered something be set up for the workers' safety. It was a huge net like the ones circus performers used.

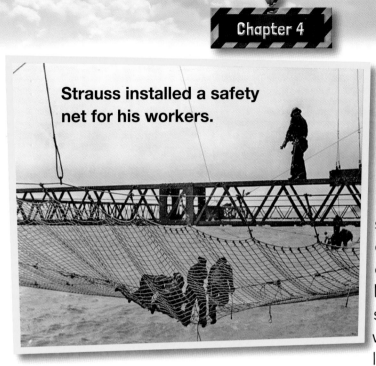
Strauss installed a safety net for his workers.

By October 1936, there had not been one serious accident. Then, on October 21, a support beam fell. It crushed a worker to death. Three months later, a heavy steel scaffold with 12 workers on it broke loose. The scaffold crashed into the safety net. Unfortunately, the net could not hold it and the workers plunged into the sea. Two men were saved, but 10 died.

Engineers checked the scaffolding to see why it had fallen. They discovered its safety bolts were too small. Those bolts were replaced with stronger, larger ones and no more workers died. Despite the tragic loss of lives, the bridge's safety net later saved the lives of 19 more workers who fell during construction. The use of a safety net was Joseph Strauss's most important contribution to safe bridge building.

Strauss's care for his workers was so respected that in 1934, workers at the port of San Francisco demanded working conditions like those of the workers on the Golden Gate Bridge.[3]

Next came the roadway. Workers hung it in sections from the cables. Approach roads for Highway 101 were built at both ends of the bridge. Each side approached equally to keep the bridge in balance during construction.

As the bridge over the strait neared completion, workers installed lights and railings. A new type of lights made of sodium vapor gave off a yellowish glow. They would help drivers see better in the fog.

Irving Morrow, the architect who designed the towers, created open railings. People driving across the bridge could enjoy views of both the Pacific Ocean and San Francisco Bay.

Paint was an important part of the bridge's construction. Salt air causes rust and corrosion, even on something as hard as steel. Paint on a steel surface can slow the corrosion process. With safety harnesses attached, painters climbed the towers, cables, and suspension cables, applying paint to every inch of the bridge.

As for the bridge's color, the military wanted it to be painted in stripes. The navy chose black and yellow, while the Army Air Corps (the name for the air force prior to 1947) wanted red and white.[4]

Morrow chose a bright shade called international orange. He knew the bright color would make the bridge stand out against the green hills of Marin County and the blue water and sky. Orange would also be easy to see in fog.

Problems arose when the painters started to get sick. Strauss ordered health exams. The workers' symptoms were strange—they could not breathe easily, felt dizzy, and their hair and teeth were falling out. Doctors discovered the workers had breathed in poisonous lead from the paint.

Strauss ordered a new type of paint be made without lead. He also insisted that workers wear breathing masks and take medicine to counter the effects of the lead. The complaints stopped, and workers stayed healthy.

The bridge was painted international orange to make it easier to see in fog.

When completed in 1937, the Golden Gate Bridge became a symbol of hope for a better life for many people.

Bridge of Hope

Work on the Golden Gate Bridge was completed on May 26, 1937. The new bridge was not just a suspension bridge, but also part viaduct and part steel arch. A viaduct is a bridge built over flat land to raise a roadway or a railroad. On both the north and south ends, the Golden Gate Bridge is a viaduct.

On the San Francisco side, an arch supports the bridge. It allows the bridge to soar over historic Fort Point, allowing both structures to stand in nearly the same place.

A big celebration was planned for Pedestrian Day on May 27, 1937. More than 200,000 people paid a nickel to walk across the new bridge. For the next seven days, parades marched on the six-lane bridge. Dozens of planes flew overhead. Fireworks exploded in the sky and bells rang in the city.

The project was even more amazing because Strauss had accepted the challenge of building the bridge for $35 million. The final cost was only $27 million.

For his efforts as the bridge's chief engineer, Strauss was paid $1 million. He was also given a gold pass, which allowed him to cross the bridge without paying a toll for the rest of his life.

On March 28, thousands of drivers paid a toll of 50 cents to drive their cars across the bridge with the longest span in the world—4,200 feet. The Golden Gate Bridge claimed that title until 1964, when the Verrazano–Narrows Bridge in New York City was built. It had a span of 4,260 feet.

The Akashi-Kaikyo Bridge in Japan has a span of nearly a mile and a quarter.

Since then, other suspension bridges with even longer center spans have been built. The Akashi-Kaikyo Bridge in Japan, built in 1998, has the longest span of any suspension bridge in the world. At 6,532 feet, it is nearly a mile and a quarter in length.

The Golden Gate Bridge has closed only three times due to gusty winds. In May 1987 it was closed a fourth time as part of its 50th birthday. On that day, approximately 300,000 people walked across the bridge.[1]

In 1989 the bridge's design was put to the test when an earthquake rattled the Bay Area. Measuring 7.1 on the Richter scale, the earthquake damaged many bridges and highways. The Golden Gate Bridge suffered no damage. Even so, inspectors added more features to the bridge to keep it safe for the future.

Strauss and the hundreds of people who built the bridge could never have imagined the number of people who would use it. By 2014, more than two billion drivers had crossed the bridge since it opened in 1937.[2] With money collected by tolls, the original debt to build the bridge was paid in the 1970s.

Each day dozens of ironworkers, electricians, painters, and other maintenance people scramble up the Golden Gate's towers and along its cables. They keep the glorious structure in good repair for the people who use it.

Over the years, the Golden Gate Bridge has become a symbol of hope. From 1941 to 1945, thousands of U.S. soldiers sailed under the bridge as they left home to fight in World War II. At the end of the war, the Golden Gate Bridge was their first welcome sight of home.

In 1996, the American Society of Civil Engineers named the Golden Gate Bridge one of the Seven Wonders of the Modern World.[3] It is featured in dozens of movies, including *Superman*, *Star Trek IV: The Voyage Home*, *Star Trek VI: The Undiscovered Country*, *Dawn of the Planet of the Apes*, and *Ant-Man*.[4]

Joseph Strauss built other famous structures, including the Arlington Memorial Bridge across the Potomac River in Washington, D.C. But he is best known for the Golden Gate Bridge, built during trying times, under harsh conditions, and in a challenging location.

On May 18, 1938, less than a year after completing the Golden Gate Bridge, Joseph Strauss died. Near the toll plaza stands a statue of him. The view of the glorious bridge in the background reminds people of what can happen when dreams and determination come together to create what others may see as impossible.

A statue of Joseph Strauss stands near the Golden Gate Bridge.

1846 Explorer John Charles Frémont names the Golden Gate Strait after a place it reminds him of in Turkey.

1870 Joseph Strauss is born in Cincinnati, Ohio.

1904 Strauss starts his business, Strauss Bascule Bridge Company.

1906 An earthquake strikes San Francisco, killing more than 3,000 people.

1917 Strauss begins researching a design for a bridge across the Golden Gate Strait.

1928 City officials of San Francisco approve Strauss's project for a bridge. They appoint Strauss as engineer in charge.

1933 Construction on the bridge begins.

1934 Longshoremen around San Francisco protest for safe working conditions like those of the Golden Gate Bridge workers.

1936 The bridge's two main cables are spun. In October, a worker dies when a beam crushes him.

1937 In February, ten workers die when a scaffold breaks and they drown. In the same accident, two men are saved from drowning. On May 26, work on the Golden Gate Bridge is completed, making it the bridge with the longest center span in the world. The next day, 200,000 people walk across the bridge on Pedestrian Day. On May 28, the bridge is open to traffic.

1964 The Verrazano–Narrows Bridge in New York City, built with a center span of 4,260 feet, becomes the newest bridge with the longest center span.

1970s Money collected by tolls of drivers across the Golden Gate Bridge pay off its original debt.

1987 The Golden Gate Bridge closes for its 50th birthday celebration. Approximately 300,000 people walk the bridge. The bridge has closed on only three other occasions, all due to bad weather.

1989 An earthquake rocks San Francisco, but the Golden Gate Bridge suffers no damage.

1998 The Akashi-Kaikyo Bridge in Japan is built. At 6,532 feet, it has the longest span of any suspension bridge in the world. Its total length is 12,831 feet.

2014 More than two billion drivers have crossed the Golden Gate Bridge since it opened in 1937.

2017 Thousands of demonstrators form a human chain across the Golden Gate Bridge in support of democracy in America.

The Golden Gate Bridge brought new opportunities for better lives for the people of California.

Chapter 1

1. *San Francisco History / Genealogy*, http://www.sfgenealogy.com/sf/history/hgpop.htm.
2. *Golden Gate Bridge. Biography: Joseph Strauss*. American Experience: PBS. http://www.pbs.org/wgbh/americanexperience/features/biography/goldengate-strauss/

Chapter 2

1. Beren, Peter. *The Golden Gate: San Francisco's Celebrated Bridge*. Earth Aware Editions, 2011, p. 22.
2. MacDonald, Donald. *Golden Gate Bridge: History and Design of an Icon*. Chronicle Books, 2008, p. 22.

Chapter 3

1. *"Golden Gate Bridge: A Technical Description in Ordinary Language."* Internet Archive. https://archive.org/stream/goldengatebridge00mens/goldengatebridge00mens_djvu.txt

Chapter 4

1. *"Safety First."* Golden Gate Bridge Highway & Transportation District. http://goldengatebridge.org/research/SafetyFirst.php
2. *Golden Gate Bridge*. The History Channel, 2005.
3. Ibid.
4. Klein, Christopher. "Six Things You May Not Know about the Golden Gate Bridge." The History Channel, May 25, 2012. http://www.history.com/news/6-things-you-may-not-know-about-the-golden-gate-bridge

Chapter 5

1. *Golden Gate Bridge*, The History Channel, 2005.
2. *"How Many Vehicles Have Crossed the Golden Gate Bridge?"* Golden Gate Bridge Highway & Transportation District. http://goldengatebridge.org/research/facts.php#VehiclesCrossed
3. *"Empire State Building."* ASCE Metropolitan Section. http://ascemetsection.org/committees/history-and-heritage/landmarks/empire-state-building
4. *"What Movies Include the Golden Gate Bridge?"* Golden Gate Bridge Highway & Transportation District. http://goldengatebridge.org/research/facts.php#Movies

Works Consulted

Beren, Peter. *The Golden Gate: San Francisco's Celebrated Bridge.* Earth Aware Editions, 2011.

Brown, David. *Bridges: Three Thousand Years of Defying Nature.* Firefly Books, 2005.

Denison, Edward. *How to Read Bridges: A Crash Course in Engineering and Architecture.* Rizzoli International Publications, 2012.

Dupre, Judith. *Bridges: A History of the World's Most Famous and Important Spans.* Black Dog & Leventhal Publishers, 1997.

MacDonald, Donald. *Golden Gate Bridge: History and Design of an Icon.* Chronicle Books, 2008.

DVD

Golden Gate Bridge, The History Channel DVD, 2005.

Massive Bridges, The History Channel DVD, 2006.

Modern Marvels, Architectural Wonders, The History Channel DVD, 2005.

Books

Cornille, Didier. *Who Built That? Bridges.* New York: Princeton Architectural Press, 2016.

Finger, Brad. *13 Bridges Children Should Know.* New York: Prestel Publishing, 2015.

Gonzales, Doreen. *7 Wonders of the Modern World.* Berkeley Heights, NJ: Enslow Publishers, Inc., 2013.

Hoena, Blake. *Building the Golden Gate Bridge.* North Mankato, MN: Capstone Press, 2015.

On the Internet

Building Big: Bridges
    www.pbs.org/wgbh/buildingbig/bridge/index.html
Fun and Learning about Bridges
    www.bridgesite.com/funand.htm
The Golden Gate Bridge
    GoldenGateBridge.org
Golden Gate Bridge
    http://goldengate.org/
National Park Service
    https://www.nps.gov/
PBS: The Golden Gate Bridge
    http://www.pbs.org/wgbh/americanexperience/films/ goldengate/

anchorage (AYN-kor-idj)—Massive concrete slab at each end of a bridge that secures the suspension cables.

architect (AR-kih-tekt)—Person who designs and supervises the construction of a building or other structure.

bascule (bas-KYOOL)—A bridge with a drawbridge that lifts to open.

bedrock (BED-rok)—The solid rock underground that supports the soil.

blueprint (BLEW-print)—A detailed diagram that shows where all parts of the structure will be placed.

caisson (KAY-sun)—Watertight chamber filled with pressurized air used in underwater construction. Caissons are left and become part of the structure.

cofferdam (KAW-fer-dam)—A temporary watertight wall used to hold back the water during construction. Cofferdams are removed once they are no longer needed.

compression (kom-PREH-shun)—A type of force that pushes things together.

corrosion (kuh-ROH-zhun)—The act of being slowly worn away.

engineer (en-juh-NEER)—A person who uses math and science to design and build things.

fender (FEN-dur)—A wall built around a bridge pier to protect it from being hit by ships.

flexible (FLEK-sih-bul)—Able to bend without breaking.

foundation (foun-DAY-shun)—A solid underground structure that supports a building, such as a bridge.

geologist (jee-OL-uh-jist)—A scientist who studies the physical history of the earth.

peninsula (puh-NIN-suh-luh)—Land that is surrounded by water on three sides and is connected to a larger landmass.

rivet (RIH-vit)—A metal pin used to fasten metal pieces together.

San Andreas Fault (san an-DREY-us FALT)—A crack in the earth's surface that runs for 800 miles south from San Francisco, California, and can be the source of earth tremors.

scaffold (SKAF-uld)—High platform on which workers can stand during construction.

span (SPAN)—Section of a bridge between neighboring supports.

strait (STRAYT)—A narrow passage of water connecting two large bodies of water.

structure (STRUK-cher)—Something made up of many parts joined together.

tension (TEN-shun)—A type of force that pulls things apart.

toll (TOHL)—A small amount of money paid by each person who crosses a highway or bridge.

truss (TRUHS)—Frame made of wood, iron, or steel beams linked together for strength.

viaduct (VAHY-uh-dukt)—A bridge for carrying a road or railroad over a highway or stretch of land.

PHOTO CREDITS: p. 1—Sage Ross; p. 8—MammaGeek; p. 12—Tewy; p. 21—Guillaume Paumier; p. 21—Ernest McGray, Jr; p. 23—Tysto; p. 25—Steven Pavlov; p. 27—Peter and Michelle S. All other photos—Public Domain. Every measure has been taken to find all copyright holders of material used in this book. In the event any mistakes or omissions have happened within, attempts to correct them will be made in future editions of the book.